Living Forgiveness

Hospitality and Reconciliation

Gordon Oliver

Director of Ministry and Training,
Diocese of Rochester

GROVE BOOKS LIMITED

RIDLEY HALL RD CAMBRIDGE CB3 9HU

Contents

The **Cover Illustration** is by Peter Ashton

First Impression June 2000
ISSN 0144–171X
ISBN 1 85174 433 9

1
Hospitality and Hiding Places

This booklet sets out to explore the opportunities and resources that could be available to help Christians in local churches deal with their consciousness of guilt and sin and receive forgiveness and healing. I believe that this opportunity needs to be a central part of the pastoral care provision of the local church. Carefully offered in hospitality and generosity of spirit this ministry could strengthen and deepen the faith of individual Christians. It would also help build up communities of faith whose members could participate more fruitfully and courageously in the God-given ministry of reconciliation which is so basic to the gospel and to Christian mission (2 Corinthians 5.16–21).

Hospitality and generosity of spirit are central to the gospel of Christ. The picture of Jesus we have in the New Testament shows him to be sure about his identity, clear about his purpose, committed to move forward in fulfilment of his calling. Yet Jesus has time for people, especially for people in need of forgiveness, healing, challenge, hope. Although he had 'nowhere to lay his head' such was the generosity of his love that even the most marginalized people—the ones his enemies write off as 'tax collectors and sinners'—find themselves welcome in his company.[1]

These are people 'with a past,' and with a present too if the truth be told. But somehow with Jesus they have no need to hide the truth about themselves. Or if they do—as in the case of Zacchaeus[2]—Jesus calls them to come out of their hiding place, receive forgiveness and healing, and live the new life of the kingdom of God.

Three key 'pictures' in the gospels are about hospitality offered to people marginalized by their circumstances or by their sinfulness. In Luke 14.12-24 Jesus tells of the 'messianic banquet' where the guests of honour will be 'the poor and maimed and blind and lame' from the streets and lanes of the city. Secondly, Jesus with his arms stretched out on the cross has often been seen in Christian art and piety as showing the loving arms of God held out to welcome the most wretched of sinners. So even here Jesus speaks the word of forgiveness, 'Father, forgive them; for they do not know what they are doing,' and assures the penitent thief of his welcome in Paradise (Luke 23.34, 43). Thirdly, after the resurrection itself Jesus restores Peter in the context of hospitality offered on a beach in the early morning. Peter ran away from the scene of the cross and there is still something in him that wants to hide. So patiently, carefully Jesus invites him to

---

1   See for example Luke 15.1–2.
2   Luke 19.1–10. Jesus' call to Zacchaeus is focused (verse 5) on his need for hospitality.

come out of his inner hiding place with the three-fold question, 'Do you love me?' (John 21.9–19).

The prologue to John's gospel characterizes the rejection or acceptance of the Word in terms of hospitality, 'He was in the world, and the world was made through him, yet the world did not know him. He came to his own home, and his own people did not accept him. But to all who received him…' (John 1.10–12).

There is a close connection in the gospels between the gift of generous hospitality and the call to forgiveness and healing in the kingdom of God. This hospitable space offered by Christ to the sinful is a space where there is no need to hide. However, Christian congregations are often places where there seems to be a lot to hide because people fear the condemnation of their friends or their pastors. The problem may be at least as much in the people doing the hiding as in deficiencies in the quality of the fellowship or the pastoral care that is on offer. People who are lonely or afraid of revealing their true feelings often do project their concerns as fantasies of what other people would think if they really know the truth about them.

Bringing Forgiveness into the Open

But that is not the whole story. For example, in many evangelical churches the preachers and teachers 'take a strong line' about particular issues of Christian discipleship, especially related to matters of personal morality. Such teaching presented in the right context and in the right kind of way can be very helpful. However, people who do not or cannot live out the 'official line' may have little option other than to keep part of themselves hidden or to leave the fellowship. Disclosure, even if the opportunity is there, can seem to be a very risky thing to do. Of course this does not just apply to evangelical churches, but the illustration is used to clarify the dynamic I am describing. A similar situation can arise where there is no clear teaching about what counts as Christian discipleship and conduct. In both cases people have to find their own ways through, or simply deny that there is any problem at all.

Clearly this kind of hiding can be dangerous for the people concerned whose spiritual vitality is likely to be progressively sapped away by their energy having to be used for containment or even concealment. But it is also dangerous for the local church as a whole. If a congregation has a lot of people in it who are keeping significant parts of themselves hidden for these kinds of reasons the spiritual integrity of the congregation as a whole, as well as of individuals, may become compromised. This must have an effect on the quality of Christian witness and mission that church can offer. On the surface all may seem well, but not far underneath are foundations built on sand rather than on the solid rock of doing, as well as hearing, God's word.

Attention to the needs of church members to have opportunities in both public worship and pastoral care settings to confess their sins and receive the assurance of God's forgiveness and acceptance places a responsibility on the church leaders. But even if they are able to seek help from their pastors, Christians with troubled consciences are more likely to receive personal affirmation, reassurance or 'counselling' than the opportunity to make their confession and receive absolution. These need not be mutually exclusive approaches, but the point is that the *routine absence of the opportunity* to seek forgiveness with the help of a trusted friend or pastor can help to dull conscience, undermine integrity and foster a sense of discouragement. As Michael Perham puts it, 'there is the danger that someone…goes away assured of the vicar's sympathy and understanding, but uncertain of the divine forgiveness.'[3]

The theological nature of forgiveness and its foundations in the character of God and the work of Christ have been helpfully surveyed by Jonathan Baker.[4] He also gives careful attention to the costliness of forgiveness both for Christ who offers it and for people who receive it. Spiritual and theological perspectives on sacramental confession have also been explored by Mark Morton.[5] But an unavoidable deficit in his approach is that he is unable to offer a clear framework or liturgy for the actual meeting of penitent with confessor except in an appendix which has a rather 'high church' feel to it. This is unavoidable, because, in spite of considerable interest in this area of pastoral care over the past fifty years, authorized liturgical texts have yet to be offered by the Church of England.

I will cover some of the same ground as Baker and Morton but from a different angle. My main attention will be on the opportunities for ministering forgiveness that already exist in our churches, and on the need to develop an approach to 'sacramental' confession that may be acceptable to evangelicals as part of the wider fellowship of the church. I write as a Church of England priest whose roots are in the evangelical tradition. I am closely involved in parish ministry, though my present job involves me in standing one step back from it for much of the time. This gives special opportunities and perspectives, as we shall see later. I believe that the ministry of reconciliation of penitents is one of real importance for all Christian groups, perhaps especially for those in the reformation traditions.

---

3   Michael Perham, *Liturgy Pastoral and Parochial* (London: SPCK, 1984) p 129.
4   Jonathan Baker, *How Forgiveness Works* (Grove Spirituality Booklet S 53).
5   Mark Morton, *Personal Confession Reconsidered: Making Forgiveness Real* (Grove Spirituality Booklet S 50).

2

Making the Most of What We Have Already Got

In Christian theology there is only one way to find the forgiveness of sin and that is through Jesus Christ. This section is concerned with ways that are already available for church members to draw near to the welcoming hospitality of Christ, 'in full assurance of faith with our hearts sprinkled clean from an evil conscience and our bodies washed with pure water' (Hebrews 10.22).

When the reformers reduced the number of sacraments to be celebrated in the newly established churches from seven to two, they took great care to ensure that those seeking forgiveness were well catered for. In the liturgies for Baptism and for Holy Communion, in Morning and Evening Prayer, and the Order for the Visitation of the Sick, the confession of sin and prayer for God's mercy are very prominent. Indeed the liturgies in the *Book of Common Prayer* have often been criticized for having too much emphasis on asking for God's mercy and too little attention to assurance of forgiveness.[6] There is some truth in this, though I suspect that further attention to discovering what God 'having mercy upon us' might mean would go some way to alleviating the problem.

When I was young I enjoyed watching wrestling on television on Saturday afternoons. When a mean looking fighter had his opponent pinned to the ground contorted in pain the underdog would cry out for 'mercy' (meaning 'do not hurt me any more' or 'do not carry out your threat'). This affected my understanding of 'Lord, have mercy upon us' when I went to church on Sundays!

Certainly we have good reason to see the connection between God's call for us to be a holy people and to live truly as the covenant people of God.[7] But the Greek words rendered 'mercy,' 'grace' and 'compassion' in the English versions of the New Testament, translate *chesed* in the Old Testament. *Chesed* carries a wealth of meaning reflecting the character of God turned toward God's people. It therefore reflects an infinitely positive reality that opens the doors to welcome reconciliation in the covenant community.

Chesed is often rendered 'mercy' but it is what you might call a positive rather than a negative mercy—it is the gift of something wonderful rather than the mere withholding of divine punishment. *Chesed* means steadfast love and faithfulness in the covenant relationship. The picture we need to see is not that of God impatiently drumming his fingers in front of the sinner, his anger only barely restrained by the death of his Son on the cross. No—the picture is of God opening his hands in generous love to welcome the sinner and offer new strength to

---

6   Jonathan Baker, *How Forgiveness Works*, p 17.
7   See Malachi 3.2

live faithfully in companionship with him. It is an essential quality of welcoming hospitality offered from the heart of God. It is *chesed* that causes the father of the prodigal to rush out to meet his son when he is still a great way off (Luke 15.20). *Chesed* as the quality of God's love freely offered in Christ is what makes it safe for the sinner to come out of hiding into the open presence of the living God.[8]

The Quest for Reconciliation

The cross is not to be seen as the ultimate picture of God's anger in the face of sin being visited on Jesus instead of on more puny fare. To put it that way sounds ridiculous, but my point is that the *internalized* picture of an ill-disposed and angry God is one that is common among both lay people and clergy in our churches and it causes untold levels of emotional and spiritual injury. This is light years away from God revealed in the living and teaching and dying and rising of Jesus Christ. If we take Jesus' own interpretation of his death, as it is represented in John, it is to be seen as the ultimate picture of how far God in his generous love will go in the quest to bring us back to him (John 15.13)—ultimate love going to ultimate lengths. The Psalmist vividly expresses the biblical idea of mercy as characteristic of God. 'Steadfast love and faithfulness will meet; righteousness and peace will kiss each other' (Psalm 85.10)—surely a picture of God's generous and hospitable welcome in reconciliation.

The purpose of this reconciliation is not simply to make the sinner feel better personally. Nor is it mainly to bring greater integrity to the community of believers, though it does both of these things. Theologically, the purpose of reconciliation of penitents is to enable them to participate once more in the life and fellowship of the covenant community of God's people. And the purpose of that community is to participate in the mission of God in the world. This is central to the message of the second part of Isaiah as he calls the exiles to accept the reconciliation God offers. 'I am the Lord, I have called you in righteousness, I have taken you by the hand and kept you; I have given you as a covenant to the people, a light to the nations' (Isaiah 42.6). These words are echoed by Simeon in prayer as he makes the connection between the covenant community and the mission of Christ (Luke 2.29-32).

Although comparatively few parishes now use the *Book of Common Prayer* for their principal services, it remains a key text for Anglican theologies of confession and forgiveness. The *Alternative Service Book (1980)* toned down the both the wording of the confession, taking some of the 'emotional hyperbole' of 1662 out and reducing the amount of prayer for God's mercy. However, although the

---

8   Many Christians use the 'Jesus Prayer' as part of their devotions, 'Lord Jesus Christ, Son of the living God, have mercy on me, a sinner.' As this prayer is repeated while we focus on the love of God in Christ, it changes 'flavour'—from the urgent petition of the penitent to the joyful affirmation of the reconciled. On this see further Keith Hubbard *In the Name of Jesus* (Grove Spirituality booklet S 72).

shapes and emphases of Anglican liturgy have changed significantly, taken to-gether their teaching about forgiveness and reconciliation is a rich resource.

Making use of what we already have in Anglican Church tradition could include the following.

a) Attention to Preaching on the Theology of Baptism and Conversion

The texts of Anglican baptismal rites, and the symbolic acts available within them give as clear a picture of conversion and the call to holiness of life as can be found anywhere. Inclusion of the renewal of baptismal vows and the welcome spoken by the congregation (another act of hospitality) opens the possibility for baptisms to be occasions for personal spiritual renewal of established Chris-tians, as well as rites of initiation for people setting out on the Christian life. The location of baptisms within main Sunday services also helps this.

Two problems concern the tendency for these rites to become routine, or (worse) regarded with hostility by established church members who may see them as interrupting the normal flow of Sunday worship, and the tendency to trivialize the rite by overmuch attention to engaging and attractive babies. These problems are increased where the candidate families are unfamiliar to the estab-lished congregation and where the attempt to make the service 'user friendly' for outsiders is taken too far. These are not easy problems to resolve. Indeed we could say that the attempt at hospitality in one direction may undermine the theological purpose of hospitality in the other. My point is simply that taking special care to ensure that the church is well taught about the connection be-tween baptism and reconciliation is one way of ensuring that good quality at-tention is given to entry into the life of grace and holiness. The symbols of the service itself, including anointing with the sign of the cross, dying to sin and rising to new life in Christ through water, passing from darkness to light, all provide opportunities for nurturing established Christians as well as for wel-coming new ones.

b) Taking Care with the General Confession in Public Worship

Common Worship follows the ASB in allowing for variations in the location of the confession within the various rites, and additionally allows for the inclusion of prayers of confession in the pastoral rites. All of the rites locate the confession in the context of preparation for or responding to the Ministry of the Word. How-ever, anecdotal evidence suggests that the prayers of confession and absolution are often highly valued by people attending church services, but also sometimes give cause for frustration and anxiety.

I suggest three reasons for these difficulties. The first is the very practical one that leaders of worship often show little sensitivity in the way they introduce the confession, either labouring the process or (more often) allowing too little space for reflection before the prayer begins. When people come to worship they very often come bearing considerable burdens and they need a space and welcome (hospitality) to lay them down and receive God's word of forgiveness.

The second reason may be that the prayers that are used seem to say too little or too much. The emotional contrast between the general confession in the BCP communion service and that of the ASB could hardly be more marked. It does seem that the more measured and cooler tone of the modern services suits contemporary (suburban) experience better for most purposes. However, for some people it may understate the burden they are bearing. Commenting soon after the publication of the ASB, Michael Perham says, 'Whether the old or the new [services are concerned], the Church must be able to find the means by which the burden of the intolerable can be worked through liturgically.'[9]

But there may be people who come to worship having no particular sin on their mind, having made a reasonable job of living a Christian life since last coming to worship. John Townroe wryly comments that when a congregation are asked to join in a confession of sins, 'Some people at that moment honestly cannot find any recent sins to confess. Their mind goes blank. Yes, they may have a general sense of falling short. But that is not actual sin, if that means a deliberate turning away from God and his will as they know it…they feel guilty for not being able to find material to be guilty about!' He asks perceptively, 'Should we expect to be committing actual sins more or less all the time? Should we not rather expect to be upheld by the power of the Holy Spirit, so that imperfect though we all are, we are kept from deliberate turning away from God?'[10]

A third, more theologically based reason, for difficulties in relation to the general confession concerns how we see ourselves as we pray the words. Who is the 'we' of the opening word of the prayer referring to? Christians in the UK have been influenced by the societal trends toward privatism and individualism in common with everybody else, and this affects the way we pray, even the way we pray liturgically. All of the Church of England confession prayers contain the word 'We.' As we might say, we the church stand *together* to confess our sins and bring our sorrow before the throne of grace. There is to be a sense of solidarity in our liturgical praying, for this is the community at prayer not just a collection of individuals who happen to be in the same place.

But there is a wider aspect as well. The community at prayer is the community engaged in mission. We pray together as people who share in the life of the world and who see the world in a particular way because together we belong to Jesus Christ. This means that the sins and sorrows of the world, as well as our own particular sins, will be significant features in the landscape of our praying. The 'liturgical menu' approach of *Common Worship*, which makes provision for a variety of ways of introducing the prayers of confession, should enable some

---

9 Michael Perham, *op cit*, p 128.
10 John Townroe, 'The Practice of Penance' in *Franciscan* Vol 11, No 1, January 1999, p 2.

real creativity and increased spiritual maturity in this respect. All of this needs to be taught and preached and explored, not only with new Christians, but also with established Christians who may have begun to take the forms and purposes of our communal praying for granted.

c) *Personal Review of Life and Prayer*

Until the mid-twentieth century the main Sunday services in most Church of England parishes were Morning Prayer and Evening Prayer. Holy Communion was celebrated very simply in the early morning and monthly following one of the other two services. In earlier times people may have participated in a Holy Communion service comparatively rarely, perhaps four times a year, normally related to the great Christian festivals. The priest gave proper notice and called upon the worshippers to engage in a time of careful personal reflection about their spiritual condition in order to prepare themselves to receive the sacrament. This call to godly reflection and examination of conscience was set in the most solemn terms. It included the requirement to consider personal attitudes toward other people, relationships with neighbours, repayment of debt, use of language about God, hindrances to God's Word, personal morality and integrity of one's own spirituality. This was a call, 'so to search and examine your own consciences, and that not lightly, and after the manner of dissemblers with God: but so that ye may come holy and clean to such a heavenly Feast…'[11]

Nowadays, when Holy Communion services are much more frequent, this kind of call is rarely given, and provision for it is not even included in the main texts of modern language services. The accent is now much more on the community meeting each other to celebrate with joy before God. The beginnings of services are often noisy as people greet one another rather than pray at that time. This may be no bad thing provided that the life of prayer is being practically encouraged, supported and actually practised away from the community's worship. But there clearly is a need to encourage Christians to engage from time to time in disciplined and carefully structured times of personal reflection and prayer about 'where they really are with God.' Some will find this opportunity in the 'rule of life' as members of the Franciscan Third Order or as oblates or companions of other religious communities. Others may find opportunities through good quality home groups. But for most the opportunity needs to be built into the programmes of teaching and prayer for both new and more established Christians. I give practical suggestions below on how this might be done.

d) *Personal Counsel and Pastoral Help*

The clear expectation in the BCP is that for most Christians most of the time the examination of conscience will lead into times of personal prayer in which

11   First Exhortation, 'Holy Communion' in *Book of Common Prayer* (CUP) p 264.

the person will repent of their sins, receive assurance of God's forgiveness, and pray for God's strength to live the new life in Christ. But some will need further support and help from their minister. In the celebrated words of the First Exhortation:

'And because it is requisite, that no man should come to the holy Communion, but with a full trust in God's mercy, and with a quiet conscience; therefore if there be any of you, who by this means cannot quiet his own conscience herein, but requireth further comfort or counsel, let him come to me, or some other discreet and learned minister of God's holy Word, that he may receive the benefit of absolution, together with ghostly counsel and advice to the quieting of his conscience, and avoiding all scruple and doubtfulness.'[12]

No formal structure was provided for this pastoral care.[13] In practice ministers would call on a fund of godly wisdom and gifts of discernment to help the person come to a place of forgiveness and peace, so that they could then, 'draw near with faith and take this holy sacrament to [their] comfort...'

Unfortunately this provision has not been clearly carried through during the processes of liturgical revision in recent years, so the existence of this opportunity is largely unknown to most worshippers and even to many clergy. The huge growth in teaching in pastoral care and training in pastoral counselling since the 1960s for both clergy and lay people does provide some opportunities for help in this direction. Most churches will have access to someone who can offer this kind of counsel, even if it is not the personal gift of the minister.[14] Rightly, personal ministry of this kind is normally offered quietly and unobtrusively. Nevertheless, unless there is explicit attention in the local church to the opportunity for confession of sin in the context of pastoral help that is offered by the church leadership, people may be left floundering or in ignorance. This also means that the in-service training provision of clergy and other pastoral carers needs to include attention to the characteristics of pastoral counselling as distinct from spiritual direction and the ministry of 'reconciliation of penitents.' But there are other factors to bear in mind too.[15]

Many lay Christians have more than one local church allegiance at the same

---

12   *ibid.*
13   The nearest the *BCP* comes to offering such a structure is the Visitation of the Sick. Although I have found no evidence of it having been used in the form in which it is written, there is a fund of wisdom there about godly living and holy dying that is well worth studying.
14   After a long period when the predominant tendency was to pathologize pastoral need and to respond to it with healing or social action strategies, attention has recently been given to finding connections between pastoral care and spirituality, with varying results, depending on the writers. A good starting point for exploring the issues would be David Lyall, *Pastoral Counselling and Spirituality* (London: SPCK, 1997).
15   Paradoxically, although the Church of England has no form for hearing confessions and offering absolution, apart from the *BCP* Visitation of the Sick, it does have strict regulations about the ministry of absolution (*The Canons of the Church of England*, Canon B29 and Canon 113 of the 1603 Code).

time. For instance, retired people may have a home in the parish but also own a caravan at the coast which they visit regularly a couple of weekends a month, and worship in that community as well as in their 'home' church. People working in cities may regularly take the opportunity to attend lunch time services or times of quiet in churches near their jobs, as well as worshipping with their families back home. There may be more direct Christian engagement going on than the 'home' pastor may be aware of. Church members might be able to take the opportunity to confess their sins somewhere else.

People may be embarrassed about the thought of approaching their own minister for this kind of help, especially if they are themselves in a position of leadership or responsibility in their own church. Disclosure of their real spiritual state to another person with whom you share regularly in close fellowship and spiritual leadership may be too much of a risk to take. So they may seek help where they can be anonymous, or at least at some distance from their normal church setting. Welcoming such people and helping them find their peace with God is a regular experience of many non-parochial clergy working in cathedrals, retreat centres and other settings.

Of course there are theological and ethical implications. Theologically, as we have seen, reconciliation of penitents is reconciliation to full participation in the covenant community of God's people engaged together in mission and witness. So even though the actual confession and absolution necessarily take place privately, every encouragement has to be given to the person to live out their reconciliation in company with their fellow church members. Often it is neither possible nor desirable to follow up the way the person is seeking to put their life in order, so this kind of approach to confession is open to abuse, but that is an inevitable risk of all pastoral ministry.

e) Attention to the Liturgical Year

The cycle of seasons and festivals in the liturgical year offers built-in regular opportunities for Christians to engage in reflection about spiritual renewal, penitence, forgiveness and the call to engage together in mission and witness. The festivals and seasons of All Saints, Advent, Christmas, Lent, Passiontide, Easter and Pentecost constitute opportunities to join the story of individual Christians and churches with the story of Jesus. This pilgrimage through the year can support a sense of purpose, form, pace and progression in discipleship in the covenant community. Creatively used it also gives a setting for interpreting what is going on in the local community and the wider world in terms of the context and agenda for mission and evangelism.

Neglect of this pattern, or insufficient attention to the integration of what replaces it, may, with other factors, contribute to a real deficit in the ministry of reconciliation exercised by the local church. The practice, fairly widespread even in Anglican parishes, of a-liturgical or semi-liturgical worship with poor levels of integration between regular patterned reading of the Bible, preaching, spirituality and mission also, in my view, contributes a major level of deficit. This may lead to a market-led rather than a mission-led church with increasingly immature levels of Christian discipleship as people shop around for the worship agenda that suits them.

My point in this section is not that we ought to hark back to some notional golden age when the church was getting these things right. Clearly there have always been problems and in any case there may be a world of difference between liturgical texts as printed and actual practice in local churches. Having ministered in council estate and industrial parishes and now living in an inner urban community I welcome the wealth of new opportunities that liturgical revision has provided. These often provide creative ways to bring the worshipping life and the witnessing life of our churches closer together. What I am suggesting is that the teaching of Scripture and the traditions of our Church provide a great deal of material to enable our reflection and practice of the ministry of reconciliation of penitents. Sensitively used, the opportunities we already have could be part of a rich resource for deepening the ministry of reconciliation of penitents.

3
Do We Need a 'Sacrament' of Reconciliation?

In this section I will argue that there is a need for a 'sacrament of reconciliation' to be part of the pastoral liturgy provision of our churches. I offer five criteria for the acceptability of a rite of reconciliation among evangelicals, then I explore where I see the need arising, and describe two possible forms such a 'sacrament' may take. Finally I will explore some practical questions which need to be considered. But first I offer a note about possible reservations that may be raised.

Among the many issues over which the sixteenth century Reformers took issue with Rome was the abuse of the rite of penance,[16] particularly the connection between confession, penance and the doctrine of purgatory with the associated issues of accumulation of merit and the sale of indulgences. The Catholic theology of priesthood was seen by them as mediation with God through representing the sacrifice of Christ and access to the means of grace only through

---

16   'Rite of Penance' was the official Roman Catholic designation of the rites which included sacramental confession before the post Vatican II reforms. The correct term now is 'Rite (or Sacrament) of Reconciliation.'

the priesthood. This led the Reformers to seeing the sacrament of penance as an instrument of social as well as ecclesiastical control in opposition to the uniqueness and sufficiency of Christ.[17]

So the idea of a sacrament of reconciliation of penitents comes with a lot of history in tow and the noises of that history have echoed down the centuries into modern times. But we are meant to grow using history as a major resource, not to be its prisoners. The highly creative way the writers of the BCP adapted a new way from earlier theology and practice suggests that within the Protestant traditions there can be room for innovation and building on more secure foundations. Furthermore, ecumenical fellowship for the past one hundred years has begun to show how the churches need to learn from each other rather than compete if we are to engage effectively in mission and ministry.

Criteria for Acceptability

Clearly, criteria for a 'sacrament' of reconciliation of penitents that could gain acceptance in reformation-based churches, such as the Church of England, would need to include at least the following five elements:

a) Firm foundation in the teaching of Scripture about repentance, forgiveness and renewal of life in Christ;
b) Clear content that encourages the penitent to meet with God in Christ, not just with the minister;
c) Declaration that God forgives and accepts the penitent (rather than the *ego te absolve* of the Roman rite and the BCP[18]);
d) Space for pastoral counsel about the new life to be offered and received;
e) Encouragement of the penitent to return into the fellowship of the covenant community.

The way that the *Pastoral Offices* have been formulated for the *Common Worship* book of the Church of England gives ground for thinking that a creative way forward may be found.[19] The *Pastoral Offices* provide core texts with variations to allow for differences of church tradition and local circumstances and are supported by 'commended material'—authorized supplementary texts which serve to advise the ministers who will lead the services. The fact that *Common Worship*

---

17 A useful brief discussion of this is found in Morton, *Personal Confession*, pp 10–15. An excellent Roman Catholic survey of the history of the rite of penance is provided by James Dallen, *The Reconciling Community: The Rite of Penance* (New York: Pueblo, 1986/1991) see especially pp 168–200. For a Roman Catholic interpretation of spirituality, theology and pastoral practice during the Reformation see Eamon Duffy, *The Stripping of the Altars: Traditional Religion in England 1400–1580* (New Haven: Yale, 1992).

18 'I absolve thee…' is included in the form of absolution in the BCP Visitation of The Sick, but has in recent years been a particular bone of contention among conservative evangelicals. Indeed, it was mainly on this point that a proposed Rite of Reconciliation failed in the House of Laity in the General Synod of the Church of England in 1983.

19 Baptism, Marriage, Funeral, Services for Health and Healing.

includes services for Health and Healing shows a responsiveness within the Church of England in reflecting growing pastoral practice and need in its provision of forms of service. I suggest that a necessary partner in this is a range of at least 'commended' orders of service for the reconciliation of penitents.

I see the need for this emerging in the following six areas of contemporary church life.

i) The Pastoral Experience of Church Leaders

The work of church leaders typically includes the ministry of individual pastoral care, often including the offer of personal counsel and spiritual guidance. Often the stories that are shared in pastoral interviews reveal unease about personal and community relationships, ethical difficulties, and elements of wrestling with temptation and sin. In practice pastors therefore find themselves 'hearing confessions' within the midst of pastoral conversations about all manner of other things. The person may need help to receive Christian teaching that speaks to their situation, reassurance that they can come to God with their concerns, help to bring their sins before God in prayer, and assurance of God's forgiveness. Pastors in these circumstances have the choice of either resorting to the Roman Catholic sacrament of reconciliation (unknown or unacceptable to many evangelicals), drawing on the wisdom of the various pastoral care handbooks, or making it up as they go along. These are highly sensitive pastoral encounters. Yet they are often drifted into, rather than being planned beforehand, and there is often an assumed rather than an explicit commitment to confidentiality. It is to the great credit of many pastors that they handle this kind of situation so well. The provision of a service of reconciliation of penitents could help focus the pastoral interview so that sin can be distinguished from other difficulties (not always easy) and offer a pastoral and professional framework for the ongoing pastoral care. This would have the advantage of clarifying *both* the reconciliation of penitents agenda and the wider pastoral care agenda. At present they are almost bound to get mixed up with each other.

ii) Evangelicals Experiencing Spiritual Direction

One result of the very welcome breaking down of barriers between church denominations and different traditions within churches toward the end of the twentieth century, is that Christians have had more freedom to learn in genuinely open fellowship with one another. Conferences, pilgrimages, quiet days, and a growing literature on spirituality have contributed. The work of major retreat centres is booming as both Christians and non-Christians engage in a renewed search for spiritual rootedness. Roman Catholic writers like Gerard Hughes and Henri Nowen have produced modern classics of writing in spirituality and became leading teachers of Christians of all allegiances.[20] Evangelicals have become alerted to the availability of spiritual direction under a whole range of titles, including 'spiritual friendship' 'soul friend,' and so on.

As evangelicals have experienced spiritual direction and begun to offer it, they have become aware of the importance of including the opportunity for confession of sin and receiving of absolution as possible parts of the helping relationship. The classic distinctions between confessor and spiritual director have begun to be recognized in theory, but generally these roles are exercised by the same people in the same settings. Again the provision of a form of service for reconciliation of penitents would be helpful in distinguishing different parts of the spiritual care agenda.

iii) Influence of the Charismatic Movement

Since the 1960s charismatic renewal has had a major influence on almost all of the mainstream churches. Positive results of this in spirituality and worship include the call for a greater sense of integration between the message preached and the *felt* experience of receiving God's word in the power of the Holy Spirit. In charismatic renewal, with its emphasis on the *experienced* work of God in the believer and the local church, the emotions and the human body are very important. There can be many problems with this, but at its best it leads to real reverence for and attention to the preaching of Scripture and high levels of commitment to practical service, as well as to lively worship. The 'invisibility factor' and 'left brain' culture of much traditional evangelicalism is challenged.

Because the human body is important, sacraments—or at least ritual signs—have also begun to play a major role in charismatic worship and pastoral care. This has made them acceptable and accessible, at least in principle, to many evangelicals who in previous generations would probably have been suspicious of them. Ritual signs such as the raising of hands in worship, the laying on of hands in prayer, anointing for healing or blessing, have become part of the common currency of charismatic worship and fellowship.

Another feature of charismatic renewal as it has matured has been an increased concern with church order, leadership and pastoral discipline. At its worst this has led to problems with 'heavy shepherding' in some independent charismatic churches.[21] But much charismatic renewal is being experienced in 'mainstream' churches where the existing leadership and authority structures are sufficiently well established and sufficiently flexible to enable a positive response. Responsible church leaders are increasingly aware of the need to give

20 For example Gerard Hughes, *God of Surprises* (London: DLT, 1985); Henri Nowen, *The Return of The Prodigal Son* (London: DLT).
21 Two important discussions of this area are Ronald M Enroth, *Churches That Abuse* (Grand Rapids: Zondervan, 1992) and Lawrence Osborne and Andrew Walker (eds), *Harmful Religion: An Exploration of Religious Abuse* (London: SPCK, 1997) see especially pp 26–42.

proper attention to the needs to church members who 'fall into sin or run into danger' and who may need the ministry of reconciliation of penitents. This combination of increased acceptability of ritual signs and regard for church order, with the commitment to biblical teaching and integrity in personal spirituality, may suggest that here too may be found fertile ground for establishing a renewed 'sacrament' of reconciliation.

iv) Needs of Anglican Catholics

While it is fairly common for anglo-catholic clergy to take spiritual and liturgical inspiration from Roman Catholic liturgical texts, and in many instances to actually use Roman rites in preference to Anglican ones, a good number of them are uneasy about doing so. This unease is certainly shared by a large number of bishops. There are broad questions of ethics and church order here, but in the case of the sacrament of reconciliation, *where no authorized alternative is available*, it is understandable that people find the resources where they can. The provision of a well-thought-through series of services for use in the Church of England would go a long way to meeting this need.

v) Services of Reconciliation Are Already Being Used

Where the Holy Spirit moves in the church to bring about new things or renew old ones, and where liturgical and pastoral structures are not available, people tend to invent new ones and wait for the official church to catch up. A clear example of this is the development of Family Services during the 1960s and 1970s. Although church groups provided forms that could be used,[22] it was nearly 20 years before 'official' texts such as *Patterns for Worship*[23] became available, and still later when 'Services of the Word' became incorporated into the mainstream liturgical provision. Whether these will be useful in family service contexts remains to be seen.

The same kind of movement is taking place in relation to celebrations of reconciliation. Increasing numbers of evangelicals are willingly taking part in 'sacramental' acts that previous generations would have found uncomfortable, such as imposition of ashes on Ash Wednesday, foot washing on Holy Thursday, celebration of movement from darkness to light at All Saints' tide, and so on. Many Christian gatherings feature 'sacramental' acts such as washing of one another's hands, individuals writing their sins on paper then burning them together within an act of prayer, and other devotional acts associated with repentance and renewal. Various groups have developed simple liturgies to support the need for structure in relation to these informal devotional acts.[24] Of course it

---

22 For example *Church Family Worship* (London: Hodder and Stoughton, 1986).
23 *Patterns for Worship* (London: Church House Publishing, 1995).
24 For example Heather Ward and Jennifer Wild, *Human Rites: Worship Resources For An Age Of Change* (London: Mowbray, 1995) see pp 16–17.

is easy to 'quench the Holy Spirit' by trying to make every creative development official. Church leaders should be encouraging creativity and freedom as well as radical faithfulness to Scripture and attentiveness to 'the great tradition.' Nevertheless, there does seem to be a need, across a wide range of the traditions of the Church of England, for some further material to be developed in relation to repentance and reconciliation.

vi) Increased Awareness of Need for Political Reconciliation

On the world stage protest and reconciliation groups have given publicity and energy to the quest for justice for the oppressed and persecuted. *The Truth and Reconciliation Commission* in South Africa brought together the victims and perpetrators of violence committed under apartheid;[25] the *Madres de Plaza de Mayo* are still calling for justice for the 'disappeared ones' in Argentina;[26] the *Stephen Lawrence Enquiry* in London has confronted racist-based murder and structural injustice, causing widespread heart searching in Christian as well as secular settings.[27] All of these groups have been and are being supported by Christian leaders.

There are also many examples of individual church leaders taking part in public acts of reconciliation. The politics of forgiveness has been briefly explored by Jonathan Baker.[28] My point here is that high-profile cases such as these, and there are many others, have begun to make congregations aware that the issues of sin, forgiveness and reconciliation must be considered more broadly than only giving attention to the pastoral needs of individuals.

This has its effect in making people more aware of the agenda of sin, forgiveness and reconciliation within more local communities and among members of congregations. In a real sense sin is back on the agenda. If it is to be put in its right perspective, room needs to be found for making the ministry of reconciliation available as a world-aware engagement in the local church. Being inspired from a distance by Christian leaders like Desmond Tutu is one thing; allowing reconciliation to come home to where we live with our neighbours in Christ is quite another. Seeing ourselves as called to be in solidarity of relationship with suffering and sinned against people in the wider world is yet another level of spirituality which the churches must foster. This all requires a renewed hospitality of ideas and attitudes, an opening of minds and hearts.

---

25   Desmond Tutu, *No Future Without Forgiveness* (London: Rider, 1999) see especially pp 206–233.
26   Leigh A Payne, *Confessions of Torturers: Reflections on Cases from Argentina* (International Forgiveness Institute, University of Wisconsin: 1998, unpublished paper).
27   John Sentamu, *The Stephen Lawrence Enquiry: Towards an Agenda for Action for the Church of England* (London: CHP, 1999).
28   *How Forgiveness Works*, pp 17–19. For a fuller treatment see Robert D Enright and Joanna North (eds), *Exploring Forgiveness* (Wisconsin University Press, 1998).

4
Celebration of Forgiveness and Reconciliation

As we consider what rites are available and the shapes that they might take in relation to the pastoral needs we have identified, there are some things that we need to bear in mind. These include pastoral need, theological background and the increasingly ecumenical character of contemporary mission. I have already suggested (page 14) five criteria that may help to make a 'sacrament' of reconciliation of penitents acceptable in reformation-based churches. Here I give the structures of two rites to measure against these criteria. The first is the Roman Catholic Rite for Reconciliation. The second is a Celebration of Reconciliation from the drafts which are still at a development stage in the Liturgical Commission of the Church of England. In both cases I will focus on the forms of the rites for reconciliation of individuals. The Roman Catholic rite is outlined first because it already exists as completed text in use.

a) The Roman Catholic Rite of Reconciliation[29]
This exists in three basic forms:
i)   Rite for the Reconciliation of Individual Penitents
ii) Rite for Reconciliation of Several Penitents with Individual Confession and Absolution.
iii) Rite for Reconciliation of Several Penitents with General Confession and Absolution.

The second two of these are variations on the first and are designed to meet pastoral need where large numbers of penitents are involved, for example at times of major festivals. The 'core rite' is that of reconciliation of individual penitents. However, the second two do lend themselves to be used with sensitivity to encourage the wider world perspective highlighted above, especially when accompanied by good quality preaching and pastoral preparation.

For convenience we will only consider the first rite. The setting is important and is designed to show the nature of the rite as a corporate celebration of the church, rather than a private arrangement between priest and penitent in a confessional 'box.' The expectation is that the rite will normally take place close to the body of the church, in the presence of other members of the congregation but that the confession environment itself will be at a suitable distance so that privacy can be assured.[30]

---

29 Published as *The Rite of Penance, Approved for Use in England, Wales and Scotland* (London: Collins 1976/84).
30 Since the introduction of he 1974 rite the use of 'reconciliation rooms' rather than the traditional 'confessional box' has been encouraged. However, old habits die hard and in large urban churches penitents often prefer the comparative anonymity of the 'box.'

The Roman Catholic Rite of Reconciliation of an Individual Penitent 1974
The Structure of the Rite is as follows:

Reception of the Penitent:	' ….the priest welcomes [the penitent] warmly and greets him (sic) with kindness'
	Greeting Sign of the Cross Invitation to Trust (verses of Scripture provided for this) Revelation of state of life (penitent shares about his Christian pilgrimage/seeking)
Liturgy of the Word	Call to Conversion[31] (passages of Scripture provided and space for brief comment)
Liturgy of Reconciliation	Confession of Sins and Acceptance of Satisfaction[32] Penitent's Prayer of Sorrow (prayers using texts from Psalms and Gospels) Absolution (with laying on of hands) 'I absolve you'
Conclusion	Proclamation of Praises of God Responsive acclamation Dismissal couched in terms of hope and healing

The range of prayers and texts offered for use in this rite give a sense of welcome, tenderness, genuineness of dealing with God in Christ, and sending forth in his name. The variety of texts offered gives to priest and penitent, at least in principle, considerable pastoral flexibility to enable responsiveness to individual need. If the hospitality of the written text is matched by the hospitality of the 'human text' in the actual celebration, here will be a rich resource indeed.

If we consider the structure and text of this rite according to our five criteria we see that: (a) its design exhibits commitment to placing the time of ministry in the setting of Scripture; (b) it calls for the penitent to bring their sins to God, not

---

31 In this context meaning the call to live the life converted to Christ.
32 'Satisfaction' here means penance and is meant to constitute the first steps toward a renewed holiness of life, a living out of conversion. It may involve particular commitment to prayer, to action, especially restitution for wrongs committed, or to service of other people.

just to the priest; (c) it takes care to minister assurance of forgiveness; (d) it contains provision for counsel toward conversion of life; (e) it looks forward sending the penitent forth to share in the life and mission of God's people.

Clearly, the *I absolve you* clause and the invitation to 'acceptance of satisfaction,' would make many non-Catholics uncomfortable. This is partly a matter of language and the way I have nuanced the satisfaction issue in footnote 32 tries to set this in a more ecumenical context. However, we still have to accept that the rite that is used has to be acceptable in the context of the church denomination and local church where it is offered. I include the rite here to show how the attempt has been made to bring together pastoral theological thinking about reconciliation with the practice of ministry.

b) Church of England Draft Developing Rites of Reconciliation[33] 'Christian Initiation, Reconciliation and Restoration.'[34]

These also take three basic forms:

i) *A Diocesan Rite* for reconciliation of one or more penitents whose sins 'have been a source of public scandal or have done grievous damage to the life and witness of the Christian fellowship.' Normally to be celebrated by the bishop during Holy Week, the penitents having been enrolled on Ash Wednesday. The penitents will be 'sponsored' and accompanied by a friend, and may be asked to abstain from receiving Holy Communion until their reconciliation.

ii) *A Parish Rite* for reconciliation of one or more penitents which may be used, 'where serious and public sin, either individual or corporate, has done grievous damage to the health and witness of a congregation or where members of the congregation have been in open hostility with each other.' Normally the rite is to be celebrated within the setting of Holy Communion after a period of preparation. The president may be the parish priest, rural dean or archdeacon, after consultation with the Bishop.

iii) *Forms for Individual Reconciliation* for use, 'when a person's conscience is burdened with a particular sin, when a person wishes to make a new start in the Christian life, or as part of a regular personal discipline.'

We can immediately see that the theology underlying these proposals sees the core rite as a corporate reconciliation presided over by the bishop and directly aimed to provide for the reconciliation of publicly known penitents and conflict groups. This has clear echoes of the early church practice of establishing penitents as distinctive groups who could prepare together with the help of spiritual directors for their reconciliation by the bishop at Passiontide or Easter. The theological accent here is on the church as the reconciling community and the key

---

33 I comment on the outline structure of these at their present state of development (April 2000) with the consent of the Secretary of the Liturgical Commission.
34 This is the working title only.

president of the act of reconciliation being the bishop.[35] The rite for individuals is to be seen theologically as a derivative of these corporate rites.

The structure is broadly similar to that of the Roman Catholic rite, with the accent on taking time for pastoral preparation and perhaps a stronger expectation that the encounter will include careful attention to the offer of 'counsel and comfort.' Certainly, if we look closely at the text and apply our five criteria the rite could in principle be acceptable to evangelicals as well as to catholics.

Draft Church of England Rite for Reconciliation of Individual Penitents
In Form 1 the structure of the rite is as follows:

Introduction	Welcome and preparation
	Verses of Scripture encouraging hope and trust in God
	Prayer for grace for the penitent
	Reading of a passage of Scripture
Confession and Counsel	Invitation
	Confession
	Priest may offer words of counsel and comfort
Reconciliation	Penitent's expression of sorrow (own words; alternative prayers are provided)
	Absolution, with laying on of hands (alternative forms provided)
	Blessing of the penitent
	Responsory, based on Psalm 103
	Dismissal

---

35 There is a tendency in writing about this and other pastoral issues to imagine a much greater uniformity of practice in the early church than was actually present. For an excellent discussion of the flux and flow of pastoral practice in relation to reconciliation during the Patristic Period see Dallen, *The Reconciling Community*, pp 29–55.

5
Three Practical Questions

i) Will These Services Actually Be Used?

This will vary with church tradition and local need. For churches where there is a tradition of confession the availability of rites of reconciliation may give increased confidence to ministers and lay people in encouraging penitence as an active part of growing discipleship. For evangelicals, I would argue that the existence of these rites will both serve as an important signal towards an area of pastoral ministry that needs to be strengthened if people are to live for Christ with integrity, and will also provide useful resources for practical use in pastoral care.

ii) Will These Rites Foster Confusion Between Forgiveness and Healing?

This is a real area of concern, but I think that the provision of rites of reconciliation will help focus the issues more clearly and will actually provide resources for discussion with pastors and 'clients' to help them recognize where the key needs lie and how to respond to them in prayer and action. A useful starting point for pastoral theology is found when we recognize that the primary Christian confession is not that I have committed such and such a sin, but 'Jesus Christ is Lord.' When we come to confess, we are in effect opening up a space for Jesus to freely be Lord where previously he has been ignored, rejected or unrecognized. The biblical words translated 'confession' have the sense of 'speaking the same language' recognizing God's version of reality as embodying the truth that sets us free.[36] The prayer for absolution is the prayer for the return of the Holy Spirit who gives the grace and strength to take our part in sharing God's life in the world.[37]

iii) Who is the Proper Minister for the 'Sacrament' of Reconciliation?

Because God in Christ is the one who forgives sin and gives the grace of renewal through the Holy Spirit, and because God is free to offer grace through any of his people, any Christian could in principle help any brother or sister to find assurance of forgiveness. In practise this happens frequently through the prayerful and sensitive offer of hospitable space and friendship. Personal confession in the secrecy of one's own prayer or sensitive pastoral sharing with a

---

36 *homologeo*: for range of meanings see William Arndt and F Wilbur Gingrich, *A Greek-English Lexicon of the New Testament and Other Early Christian Literature* (Chicago: University of Chicago Press,1957) p 571.
37 Two good quality sensitive discussions of these issues are Mary Anne Coate, *Sin, Guilt and Forgiveness: The Hidden Dimensions of a Pastoral Process* (London: SPCK, 1994) see especially pp 152-190 and Philip Yancey *What's So Amazing About Grace?* (Grand Rapids: Zondervan, 1997).

friend are often all that is required.

However, the 'sacrament' of reconciliation is intimately linked with Christian initiation, with reconciliation of the sinner to God and to fellowship with God's people. Therefore this is a question about ecclesiology as well as about personal pastoral care. For this reason the most appropriate minister will be one who is able to fulfil the role of presidency at the eucharist. Ideally this ministry is exercised as part of the collaborative ministry and mission of the local and the wider church, so lay people should also be involved where possible, particularly as friends and supporters of the penitents.

Wherever it is offered the proper structures of that church must be observed. A formally offered rite 'sacrament' of reconciliation only makes sense if it is made available as part of the hospitality of creative sacred space, and that can only be 'owned' by the church, not by any individual in it. In any case, such is the depth and sensitivity of this ministry that it must be exercised by spiritually mature people who are themselves prepared to accept their own need to seek reconciliation with God in Christ as well as to offer this opportunity to others.

Desmond Tutu comments, 'True forgiveness deals with the past, all of the past, to make the future possible.'[38] Being called to share as friend or minister in the reconciliation of penitents means being called to the generous hospitality that opens wide the door to welcome this part of God's future.

38   Desmond Tutu, *No Future Without Forgiveness*, p 228.